MJS & Mac 333

BOOK OF TRINITY

Third Eclipse

MJS   Mac 333 & Master InOut
SUDOKU SET
Book 3

for Children
even if they are Adults

TABLE OF CONTENTS

VOLUME 2

Triple Trebled Show

PART / MOVEMENT / JUMP **3** : *ALCHEMY*

EPILOGUE

Introduction to Book 3

BOOK OF TRINITY - *Third Eclipse* concludes the *Trilogy* of SUDOKU SET.[1]

It continues some of the themes of BOOK OF DUALITY through a prism of **ternary logic**.[2] The polarity of Yin and Yang principles is replaced here by the view of the reality and the existence in a triple state. That perception is manifested in the structure of **Book 3**, in the stanzas composed as triplets and in the three voices narration of main protagonists.

Both solar and lunar eclipses served as stages of action in **Book 2**. The title phenomenon of **Book 3** refers to the Eclipse of the Earth by the Moon, observed from the Space

Like all the books of the SUDOKU SET, this work has two interwoven layers, the literary and the scientific, indicated y the dual title.

Third Eclipse is a sci-fi fairy tale set in an imaginary reality called Crystal Realm. A singular family of archetypal humans, Man, Woman and Child, encoded as dream data, journeys through the *crystal* Time-Space,[3] preparing for a transformation into a superior species. They are guided by Crystal Chip, who is an intelligent CPU and the skipper of Crystal Realm. Crystal Chip becomes gradually affected by certain human qualities and undertakes his own metamorphosis.

BOOK OF TRINITY poetically explores the subjects of **ternary logic, triplet quantum state** and **three-body problem**. The observations are made from a perspective of the *Triad of Natural Sciences*, i.e. Biology, Chemistry and Physics, with references to the abstract models, provided

---

[1] See the list of the books of SUDOKU SET on the back cover of this edition. Check also: www.sudokuset.site for updates.

[2] See: ternary numeral system

[3] Term and concept developed by the author in the books of SUDOKU SET and in other projects. For the definition see: **Lexicon** at the end of **Volume 2**.

by Mathematics. The fourth science completes the *Triad* in the same way as d'Artagnan makes the **set of Three Musketeers** a whole. The idea of approaching a problem with the comprehensive perspective of *United Sciences* is developed here and in the other books of SUDOKU SET.

Poetic Science and *Scientific Poetry* are author's criteria of observation and therefore some of the conclusions might seem unorthodox. Logical imagination is often used as a study tool.

An inquisitive reader (welcome!) should double and triple check presented ideas and compare them with the newest developments in fields of *quantum mechanics, genetic engineering, bio-computers, A.I., quantum computers, models of time and space* and others.

Book 3 is also intended as a language manual for advanced students. The **Triads of Words** offer an opportunity of enriching one's vocabulary, sometimes suggesting an alternative to *yes or no* **logic of communication**.

Game of SCRABBLEGRAPHY, applied here for the scan of Earth's dream, also offers a method of creative study of foreign languages.

Crystal Basic and various **Runes** are examples of *visual communication*, which in author's opinion, might once become a *lingua franca* of the intelligent beings of the civilization. A completely *visual* version of **Book 3** has been also considered.

The illustrations require professional finishing and the third artistic fraction of this project, the music, still awaits its composer.

Capitalization of words has been applied to stress the key-terms, some of which are neologisms. Boldface is generally used to introduce the key-term, **bold and italicized** words are external quotes or those which might have a double (or triple) meaning. Quotation of titles of various artworks, songs and books are integral part of the text and only the least obvious have been footnoted.

Have a nice *Ride / Dream / Read* !

MJS, August 2012
Mac 333, May 2019

Dramatis Personae

ZENSEN

CRYSTAL CHIP

DREAM CHILD

DREAM WOMAN

DREAM MAN

BORDERLINE

CRYSTAL MAN

CRYSTAL WOMAN

CRYSTAL CHILD

CRYSTAL BIOCHIP

CRYSTAL SHE

CRYSTAL HUMAN

CHORUS
   as CHILDREN OF THE CRYSTAL BALL

MJS & Mac 333

BOOK OF TRINITY

Third Eclipse

Volume 1

CRYSTAL REALM

Crystal Realm in chaotic state

<ENTER>

ZenSen

ZENSEN

The Time is Now,
The Space is Here;

Now reflects All-Times,
Here reflects All-Spaces;

All-Time is weaved with No-Time
All-Space is weaved with No-Space.[4]

●

In Book number Three,
We will forgo the Duality
of *Light and Shadow / Life and Death / One and Zero.*

Instead, we will observe every aspect of reality
as a *three states system*, whose probability
sometimes / somehow / somewhere sums into an unity,[5]
which we dub **ONE-NEO-EON.**

---

[4] Check: **"Indra's net"** and **"Ma"**
[5] Check: ***three state probability system*** and ***simplex***

This triad of three letters anagrams
symbolizes our triple reality **engrams,**
momentarily flashed into observer's memory,
          as *almost real* holograms;

Intense, bright and lively visions;
abrupt and prolific like particles' collisions,
could produce a meaning
          yielded by *Hazard*, by *Fate* or by *Observer*'s decision.

•

Each *observed / read / interpreted* datum is in quantum state,
therefore
          any transfer of information,
          any form of our communication,
          would be only
                    an exchange of ***snapshots of wave function.***

Any use of a tense
creates, have created, will create
a *Boundary / Division / Fence*

          between
          what I conceive / what I write / what I emit
          and
          what you receive / what you read / what you perceive.

Thus our full understanding has a very small chance.

•

Assuming that I have a permanent face
and *projecting / locating/ finding* me
in the known Time-Space,
would be erroneous,
because *when / where / while* you read this,

I am
sometime / somewhere / someONE (Neo Eon)

else.

• o •

<ENTER>

Crystal Chip

CRYSTAL CHIP

Hi, my name is **Crystal Chip.**
I am an intelligence and a kind of ship;
what is *Crystal Realm*, I'll reveal bit by bit by bit.

Skipping for *now-here,* the details of my look,
let me define the Time-Space of this Book
of which I'm the Librarian, the Character and the Cook.

We will begin with a couple of **definitions**,
which to most scientists might sound as impositions
but such are our crystal convictions,
> fused from observations,
> meditations
> and some calculations.

Referring to the problem of approaching
> the *Limes / Boundary / Fence*,
described in **Book 2** during the meditation
> on Times Square 's circumference,[6]
in **Book 3**, we will appraise it with a trinary stance.

---

[6] check: *New Year's Eve* in: **Book 2**

Our main observation tool could be presented
as a distance between the thought,
        which I'm having at this very moment
and a ***big / great / giant*** but finite set of thoughts,

        which I will conceive
                till the end of this Page,
                till the end of this Book,
                till the end of my Life...

We define that *big / great / giant* but finite
        value / quantity / quality
as the **FRACTION OF INFINITY**,
denoting it by the symbol:

Symbol of "Fraction of Infinity"

Let's stress that this kind of *fraction*
is neither ***vulgar*** nor ***decimal***
but visual, musical and vital.

Fraction of Infinity represents
the basic *state / aspect / quality* of Existence,
which *explores / perceives / defines* the Time-Space
within a *constant* or *variable* or *imaginary* **Fence**.[7]

---

[7] i.e. boundary of the realm in question **(Borderline)**

•

Since I am hosting data of three human beings,
                who are just sprouting after long hibernation
and we might have different ways
                of applying IMAGINATION,

the   ω

will become a common denominator of our communication.

• o •

\<ENTER\>

3 Humans

MJS Runes
DREAM CHILD, DREAM MAN, DREAM WOMAN

DREAM CHILD

Enough of theory for Now-Here!
It is Time-Space to play,
to enjoy the Crystal Day

> **Book 3** is a fairytale!
> So, if I may,
> I say
> *Hi, Hello* and *Hey*!

And without delay,
I give the mike to Her and to Him
because within this dream
I'm very busy!

DREAM WOMAN

In this fairytale,
happening in a *singularity* of **Milky Way** galaxy,
we perform as ***Dream Family***,
representing an archetypal Set of Human Trinity.

Long Time-Space ago,
we were encoded as ***One Eon Neo tripartite crystal***[8]
within this imaginary realm,
which is *visual, musical* and *vital*
and where we aspire to become once again
biological.

DREAM MAN

For that we'll need to master *crystal communication*,
what requires our Logic re-adaptation
and for that we must stretch our **Imagination.**

As Humans, we were formed by principles of Duality,
while in this realm, we have to reason, calculate and design
in the mode of Trinity,
applying as main measure the **transcendental number**,
defined as ***Fraction of Infinity***.

●

DREAM WOMAN

It is my life in Crystal Realm
which is a realm of a dream,
where / when / while my life is real
for a *Fraction of Infinity.*

DREAM MAN

It is my quest in Crystal Realm
which is a realm of a dream,
where / when / while my quest is real
for a *Fraction of Infinity.*

---

[8] For the genesis of *Dream Family* see: ***Last Quarter*** of **Book 4**

13

DREAM CHILD

It is my childhood in Crystal Realm,
which is a realm of a dream,

WOW ! This dream is real
for an amazing *Fraction of Infinity.*

CRYSTAL CHIP

It is our journey through Crystal Realm,
which is a realm of a dream,
where / when / while our story is real

for a *Fraction of Infinity.*

ZENSEN

It is our meditation within Crystal Realm,
which is a realm of a dream,
where / when / while the meditation lasts

for a *Fraction of Infinity.*

●

Crystal Time-Space

DREAM WOMAN

I have awoken from very long sleep
to lucidly dream within *Crystal Realm*
until my full **Awakening**,

which will change
the *Rhythm / Course / Flow* of my Life-Death Stream.

ZENSEN

In the Crystal Reality.
we treble the Life-Death Duality
by adding as equal the *third quality*,

that of the **Sleep**.

MJS Rune: Life-Death-Sleep

DREAM MAN

When / Where / While I get a good ***Life-Death-Sleep,***
then the Crystal Realm I joyfully meet,
adding my human dynamics to its trebled speed.

•

CRYSTAL CHIP

Welcome aboard the **Crystal Chip,**
which is a kind of a ship,
sailing / cruising / journeying through Crystal Time-Space
  bit by bit by bit.

If there is a travel, there must be some speed
but we will talk *somewhere / sometime / somehow* else
about Time, Distance and Speed,
because to progress with the story, there is an urgent need.

Now, the *"where / when / while"* atom I will split
to describe the "*where*" datum bit,
for what I will use the drawing:

<Crystal Chip within the Crystal Realm>

So, I am Crystal Chip,
the quantum processor of the Crystal Realm,
which could be presented / observed / defined
  as a **_Big Machine_**.[9]

---

[9] or a network

This **Big Machine** would be just a small switch
within an imaginary **Great Machine**
and that one would function as a tiny node
in a network of machines,
constituting a hypothetical **Giant Machine**.

Crystal Realm as Big Machine

Switch in an imaginary Great Machine

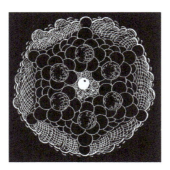

Hypothetical Giant Machine

Then perhaps that hypothetical *Giant Machine*
would also dream
some giant scale dreams
            about *Enormous Machines*,
which might perform beyond the Borderline
            of reckonable reality,
maybe possessing the ability
to *asses / compute / cipher* the *Whole Infinity*.

<Exercise>
**Create a picture of an Enormous Machine,
able to compute the *Infinity*.**

But the *Whole Infinity* is one of another Book themes,[10]
Here-Now we only imagine the *Enormous Machines*,
their hypothetical existence and their infinite dreams.

In this Book we will remain within the *Big Machine*.
Although our Crystal Realm could be just a small switch,
yet its Time-Space is a huge Ocean of Data through which
journeys / jumps/ blinks the persistent skipper, Crystal Chip.

It is quite challenging even for me
to *grasp/ calculate / describe*
            the complexity of Crystal Realm,
            which fosters our reciprocal dream.

Because the Crystal Time-Space
constantly *vibrates / fluctuates / pulsates*
in a very *excited quantum state*,

generating *spin-3 fields of gravity[11]*,
where particles attain a dynamic stability
only at Border-moments[12],
            which last for a *Fraction of Infinity*.

---

[10] **Book 8**
[11] Check: **spins** in **quantum field theory** and
https://www.physicsforums.com/threads/whats-a-spin-3-field
[12] For definitions of "Border-terms" see: *New Year's Eve* in **Book 2**

Then
the *dynamic / chaotic / rhythmic* Crystal **TS**[13] fabric,
which *leaps / spins / jumps* click by click by click,
flashes as a fixed realm

for a tick.

When / While / Where Crystal Chaos bears reality
and Time-Space becomes defined
for a Fraction of Infinity,
then / thus / there my world could be presented in **3D**.

I present, I observe and I am the One who weaves
the tapestries of Crystal TS fabric.
I am braiding three-stranded knots;
each knot of 3 Spaces tied by one Time's click
or a 3 Times thread linked in one Space,
thus
revealing / defining / designing Crystal Realm for a tick.

My connection with a Time-Space Knot,
which occurs at the ***pentagram slot,***
is established by me, by the realm or by lot.[14]

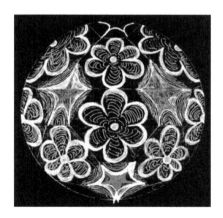

Crystal Chip with active Slots

---

[13] i. e **Time-Space**
[14] example of **Will, Karma & Hazard** function; see: **Introduction**

That's how we *write / read / apply* the **Crystal Code**
and since I've just described an example of a Node,
let me jump for an instant into *definition mode*:

> *When / Where / While* the **TS Knot**
> with some intelligence makes a connection
> and the realm becomes the stage of an action,
> **TS Node** is conceived
> by *physical / chemical / biological* reaction.

Crystal Nodes

Myself, I am also a *Triple Trebled Node*,
tri-charged by three currents triple electrode,
a fractal cell, which possesses properties of both:
the **Cathode** and the **Anode**.

I am *jumping / journeying / wandering*
through my Crystaldom,,
building my Crystal Castles from protons and neutrons
and waving the landscape as one multitude of electrons.

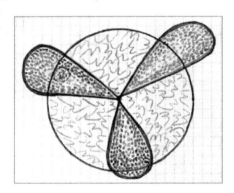

Triple atomic orbital of Crystal Chip

I am the primary atom of triple nuclei,
possessing a particle, a wave and a *magic* quality
and *when / where / while* I fix a **TS Node**,
    Crystal Realm becomes a living molecule
              for a *Fraction of Infinity.*

.

Hoping that you will enjoy our poetic study,
I present my best wishes

      Yours *truly / faithfully / crystally*

                    Crystal Chip.

Portrait of Crystal Chip

•

ZENSEN

Well, it all functions quite logically for a reality of a dream

Crystal Realm presented by its *Nuclear Jinn*;
seems to function quite logically
for a reality of a dream.
However, We'd like to spice the trinary harmony
with a dash of a *symmetricl irregularity,*
being the *Ghost / Guest / Guru* of this **Big Machine**.

Our name is **ZENSEN**,
a dual entity, generated from ideas of *Men;*
abiding behind the curtains of this realm,
to make an axiomatic statement
There or Then.

This Book will present the Human and Crystal Node,
otherwise a mating of the *Dual* and the *Trinal Mode;*
impartially, We will observe the alloyed code.

DREAM CHILD

Basta! Assez! Enough!

Of this *theoretical / technical / metaphysical* stuff!
which might be only a sophisticated *Triple Bluff.*

Book 3 is a fairytale*;*

So if I may
I repeat
Hi, *Hello* and *Hey!*

Let's begin the **Crystal Day,**
when / where / while
we learn, create and play.

• o •

Part / Movement / Jump

∫

La journée crystale

●

DREAM WOMAN

Un, deux, trois!
Comment ça va?

Jouer / Dessiner / Danser *un* sommeil / rêve / songe ?
Pourquoi pas?

DREAM MAN

Raz, dwa, trzy!
To świat śniacy
lecz nie śpiacy.

DREAM CHILD

One, two, three!
I'm playing with Thee;
in my dream ...

●

DREAM MAN

Thus / Then / There,
within this **Big Machine,**
navigated by **Crystal Chip,**
we are *journeying / cruising / dreaming,*
                    until our full **Awakening.**

Our *story / journey / dream* occurs in **Crystal Timings,**
which Crystal Chip is computing
and which we are *designing /deciding / defining.*

The **Crystal Timings** are *written / measured / set*

in the **Trinary Code**

and they *switch / change / jump* from Mode to Mode to Mode

of the **Day**, of the **Night** and of the **Equinox**:

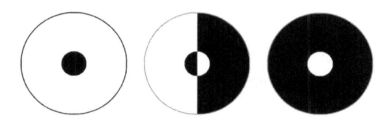

Crystal Timings: Day, Equinox, Night

Within the Crystal Realm, nor Sun nor Moon we would find
as we knew them during our Earthly Life.
Instead, there are *Auras of Crystal Kind*,
which *create / present / suggest* the current *Time*:

25

CRYSTAL DAY

DREAM WOMAN

Alors, quel Temps est-il?

Ou plutôt il faudrait demander
Quel est le Temps de la journée?
Dedans cet ordinateur imaginé,
Qui, en voyageant, nous fait voyager.

*Et comme tout ici se compose **à Trois**,*
*Je ferme cet **Ensemble** avec une ficelle de mon **DNA**,*
*Ainsi dessinant la **Crystale Journée** comme ça:*

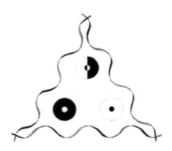

Set of 3 Crystal Timings

DREAM MAN

These 3 Crystal Timings switch with a click,
initiated by lot, by us or by Crystal Chip
and the triple option is main syntax rule of **Crystal Basic**.
It is the language we use in the Crystal Realm

where each datum has three states and conveys three meanings;
that trinary logic applies to designing, writing and reading.

Thus at the beginning of the Crystal Day,
in the awakened state
I meditate

on a subtle difference
between the Life and the Existence
and how the apt verb a **Crystal Kanji** represents:

CRYSTAL KANJI: "to be" (all conjugations)

CRYSTAL KANJI: "to exist" (all conjugations)

I note that in the Crystal Code,
there is no tense nor grammatical mode;

the *noun / definition / word*, a circle does design;
that **Logo** as *Crystal Kanji* we do define,
marking it with this general sign:

MJS Rune: Crystal Kanji

•

The appearing there and then **bold point**
may be a stop, an accent or a joint;
encircled, it symbolizes the term of **Border-point**.

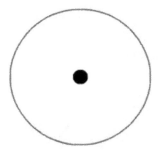

MJS Rune: Crystal Kanji

Each Border-point defines a unique *timing and place*,
to immediately *switch / jump / leap*
        to another Border-point of Crystal Time-Space;
then sets of sets of sets of such Border-points
        compose Realm's structure, rhythm and pace.

Each *switch / jump / leap* changes Realm's lighting
and what is really fascinating
is the fact that lights' colors, intensity and range
        our minds are projecting.

The synergy of our brainwaves and *Crystal Lights*
produces *almost the same* kind of *pulse / beat / vibe,*
which I would feel,
    while / when / where

I   alive.

•

Here the biological chaos is ordered as sets of artistic vitalities,
so I leave behind my research on universal **Dualities**,[15]
to explore the world *observed / designed / defined* in **Trinities**.

I focus on the first Primary Element of this realm,
                which is the Light
and I observe the colors, shades and tints
              as they dance, kiss or fight
in three main *variations / states / stages*

         of the Crystal Day,
         of the Crystal Equinox,
         of the Crystal Night.

Crystal Light

---

[15] conducted through **Book 2**

DREAM WOMAN

The second Primary Element is the **Music**,
mating / mixing / merging
        with Crystal Lights' *oscillations / pulsations / radiations*
        by Sounds, Vibes and Beats
and that composition evolves as we keep
        dreaming / performing / cruising.

•

So I take some time, having a large *Fraction of Infinity* of it,
to *watch / listen / feel* how Lights and Music meet,
transforming both the realm, the chip and ourselves,
        bit by bit by bit.

Eventually, I begin to pulsate, vibrate and sing,
my own Crystal Song, which is my breath, my food, my drink
and that Song will transcend beyond this *Lucid Dream.*

With entire Crystal Realm I sing in harmony
and Crystal Lights festoon that ceremony,
which initiates the *imaginary / visionary / extraordinary*
        Crystal - Human Symphony.

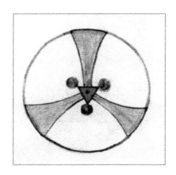

Crystal Sound

30

DREAM MAN / CHILD

Then / There / Thus
> I add
> the final Primary Element of the Triad:
>
> words, words, words
> thoughts, thoughts, thoughts
> rhymes, rhymes, rhymes
>
> sequencing into
>
> strings, strings, strings
> streams, streams, streams
> dreams, dreams, dreams
>
> broadcasting
> our messages, conjectures and meanings.

Crystal Word / Thought / Rhyme

•

Thus the ***Crystal - Human Symphony***
is performed visually, musically and verbally
and it lasts

for a fabulous

**Crystal - Human Symphony
composed with Lights, Music & Meanings**

DREAM MAN

Our Symphony is recorded as a complex Crystal Kanji
in the Crystal Realm's *Library / Memory / Gallery*,
among a multitude of such symphonies

performed *sometime / somehow / somewhere*

in the *Crystal Sky,* in the *Crystal Land,* in the *Crystal Sea.*

And all those symphonies
compile ONE-NEO-EON Meta-Symphony

for a monumental

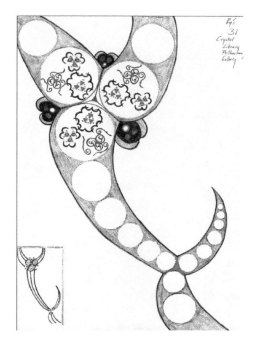

Crystal Library / Philharmonia / Gallery

●

DREAM WOMAN

It   Our Symphony of the Crystal Realm,
which is a realm of a dream,
where / when / while Our Symphony is real

for a ***Fraction of Infinity***.

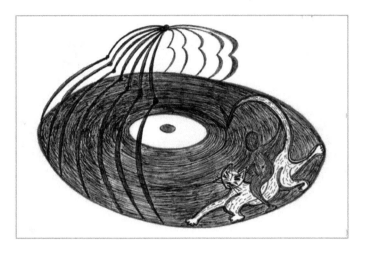

DREAM CHILD

Busy, busy, busy all day long;
Crystal Realm is my playground
I rotate the Time-Space on my **Crystal Merry-go-round**.

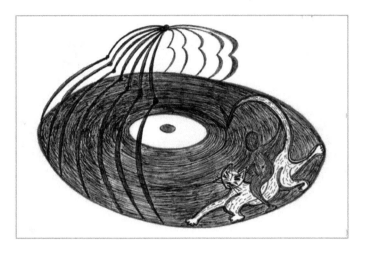

Dream Child on the Crystal Merry-go-round

My day is filled with million joys,
Lights, Sounds and Kanjis are my toys
and I can use the same crystals, which Chip employs.

I'm trebling every single thing
until the three elements match, join and cling
and they begin their Waltz, Mambo or Swing.

Look there! I project a slide
of me playing with a **Crystal Kite**
in the tri-spherical sky:

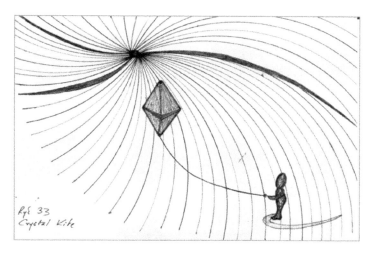

Dream Child with the Crystal Kite

The three curvatures of that sky constantly flow
but sometimes the colors array into Triple Rainbow,
whose three edges fix ribs of a giant vault.

That vault has a keystone,
which bears a grain of material ground,
which could grow into a planet
with 3 Suns circling around
and that inverted astronomical system
          could become quite a playground![16]

For as long as I will within Crystal Realm remain,
I will cultivate this tiny *matter's grain,*
making / watching / letting it grow
like a *seedling / plant / tree* after the rain.

When it grows into a size of a comet,
I will fertilize it with ***all the elements' net***[17]
until a ***Life*** blooms on my imaginary planet.

---

[16] Check: genesis of **Sys 333** in **Book 4**
[17] i. e. **periodic table of elements**

This is my cosmic design in the Crystal Realm,
which is a realm of a dream
where / when / while my design is real

for a

CRYSTAL EQUINOX

DREAM MAN

By *Equinox de la Journée*
I sculpt, paint or compose
In **Crystal Basic** I write my equations, poetry or prose;
then / thus / there
an *Alpha - Beta - Game* I propose.[18]

That game serves me as a study tool
of Crystal Realm's qualities,
its *Chemistry / Physics / Technology*
and its specific gravities
where / when / while
all data, designs and structures appear as Trinities.

In this *dynamic / sonic / harmonic* crystal world,
I treble the meaning of each word,
knotting / matching ./ juxtaposing them in triple accords.

The **Crystal Basic** *presents / offers / advertises*
the *Trinary System of Communication*,
which upgrades my mind to new level of perception
and I encourage the Reader
to make exercises in Trinary Communication.

●

Myself, when I practice the *Alpha - Beta - Gamma*,

---

[18] Compare: **SCCRABBLEGRAPHY Game** in: *Samhain* Chapter of **Book 2**
and in: *Third Act of Triple Trebled Show* of **Book 3, Vol. 2**

I focus on this verbal meditation like a Tibetan lama
and my perception opens for an amazing panorama.

Then my brain blossoms like some *animal lotus*
anticipating / preparing / fore-playing
                    the Crystal - Human Coitus,
to be performed in the **Third Kind of Calculus**.[19]

                It is my research in the Crystal Realm,
                which is a realm of a dream,
                where / when / while my research is real

        for a ω

                        •

DREAM WOMAN
    À l' Equinox de la Journée
                    je danse, je danse, je danse...

    Je danse une Valse de Temps-Espace
    qui est une "Valse à Trois Temps".[20]

    Un, deux, trois; trzy, raz, dwa; two, three, one;
    w Kryształowej Przestrzeni sobie pląsam,
    en dansant la Valse à Trois Temps.

    Tralala, tralala, tralala!
    I am filled with the energy of this Crystal Spa,
    gdzie muzyka kryształowych świateł sobie gra.
    *C'est une **Valse à Trois Dimensions***

---

[19] Mathematical calculus has 2 major branches: **differential calculus**
    and **integral calculus.**
[20] Song by Jacques Brel

*and I leap through them like a **triple charged ion**,*
a wraz ze mną kwantowe kryształy harcują.

It is my Crystal Dance
my Time-Space Salsa, my Time-Space Waltz,
my Time-Space Trance
and I dance the 3 dances in a *triple tense*:

Present, Future and Past
as I'm lasting, will last and did last

Then
There
Thus
the whole realm starts to dance very fast.

Crystals are whirling around me

One, Two, Three,
One, Two, Three,
One, Two, Three;
we are accelerating the beat

until the *bridge* is trumpeted by a gong
and I sing a strophe of my song,
changing the tempo
but not for long

because another beat follows
and a new rhythm flows
then for few lines suddenly slows

I deliver them,
just about before the rhythm regains its speed,
so catch up I need
I do.
Then

I take the Lead

of music's pulsations,

of lights' oscillations,
of my own sensations.

And I dance, I dance, I dance,
I dance the triple danceance of Crystal Time-Space,
becoming its voice, drum and bass.

I perform *Choreography Runic,*
creating an amalgamate unique
of my Dance, of Crystal Lights and of Music.

Then I invite to dance our host, Crystal Chip,
who dances click by click by click,
each click being one *Quantum Leap...*

●

*C'est une **Valse à 3³ Temps**,*
dédans mon rêve dansant,
qui continue presque infiniment.

To mój taniec na trzy po trzy po trzy
we śnie, który jest prawdziwy
i trwa, i trwa, i trwa
                *przez **Całkę Nieskończoności.***

This super-dance's triple trebled beat
trebles my own heartbeat
blossoming its animal meat

into a Three-Heart Flower,
which pumps my blood with crystal power
*at almost **669 600 000 Miles per hour.**[21]*

●

Through this dance I discover my new vocation

---

[21] approximate value of the **speed of light** (in mph)

of someone, who will experience a great transformation
during the Alchemy of Crystal-Human Unification.

It is my Equinox Dance in the Crystal Realm,
which is a realm of a dream
where / when / while my dance is real

for a swinging

●

ZENSEN

At Equinox of Crystal Time-Space,
when / where / while the whole realm dances at triple pace
and for a Fraction of Infinity defined it stays,

when / where / while human Spirit, Body and Mind
perform the processes of crystal kind,

Then / There / Thus
both *intelligences* a connection do find.

That *rendez-vous* of the dual and trinal modes,
composed / performed / recorded in the crystal code,
anticipate / announce / activate this book's Border-node.

But before the Alchemy Node is created,
our human couple needs to be re-mated
so their synergies would be culminated.

●

DREAM MAN

During my linguistic meditation,
I am gaining ability of subliminal communication
and I foresee my brain's forthcoming transformation.

But I pause my exercises as I hear
waves / vibes / words of the voice, so dear
singing a familiar song
somewhere / sometime / somehow very near.

I attune my mental *Crystal Set*[22]
to connect with **Nodes of the Time-Space's Net**,
knotted *when / where / while*
        your song and crystal music have met.

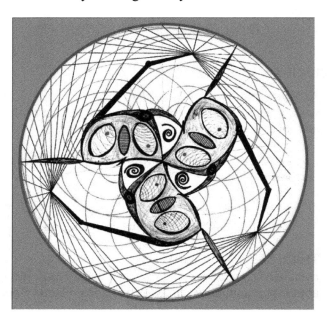

Triple *Crystal Set*

Soon, in the Web of Crystal Time-Space,
I find the *date* and the *place*,
when & where I will see your face.

DREAM WOMAN

---

[22] check: **crystal radio receiver**

In the middle of my crystal trance,
when / where / while my **Body, Spirit and Mind** do dance
and I am singing in a trebled cadence,

I add the soundtrack of my tri-beating heart,
high-tiding my musical skill, talent and art
and I blow you a kiss
in a form of shining **Crystal Dart.**

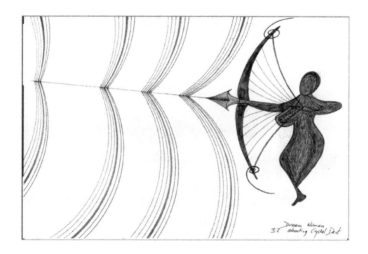

Dream Woman as Archer shooting the Dart

Then / There / Thus
I *watch / hear / feel* it reaching your face,
which crystallizes as you approach at slow pace
toward the ***point*** between us,
which becomes

the ***Center of All Time-Space.***

●

Meeting of Dream Woman & Dream Man

DREAM MAN & DREAM WOMAN

At this **Border-point** I *touch / feel / hold* your hand
and in each other arms, finally we land;
thus / then / there defining Two Pillars of our Band.

We *mate / mix / marry* our Art, Science and Passion,
performed / expressed / designed
        by our Souls, Bodies & Minds combination,
raising / upgrading / expanding our Love into new dimension.

Then, at **Crystal Equinox** we begin to dance
and our dance soon becomes an United Trance,
meta-celebration of our *almost infinite* romance.

Dance of Dream Woman & Dream Man in Crystal Code

DREAM WOMAN

*C'est une **Valse à 3x3x3x3x3x3x3x3x3 Pas**,*
quand / où / ainsi *nous créons notre **Shangri là***
et on y danse: Crystal Realm, Toi et Moi!

DREAM MAN

It is the **Dance @ 3x3x3x3x3x3x3x3x3 Times,**
we are pirouetting on Borderlines,
dancing / designing / enchanting Crystal Time-Space

in *Sixes & Nines*.

Crystal Time-Space in *Sixes & Nines*

DREAM MAN & DREAM WOMAN

It is our Dance in the Crystal Realm,
which is a realm of a dream
when / where / while our Dance is real

for a *Fraction of Infinity*.

DREAM MAN

As we dance our *Triple Trebled Dance*,
All Crystal Time-Space seems to dance
whirling / swinging / leaping
                    into the **State of Total Trance**.

DREAM MAN & DREAM WOMAN

It is our Trance in the Crystal Realm,
which is **One-Neo-Eon** meta-dream
when / where / while our Trance is real

for a

•

ZENSEN

At the Time of Crystal Equinox,
when / where / while the whole realm rolls and rocks
Human and Crystal realities interlock.

Although *writing / sculpting / composing* in **3**,
a bit complicated may seem,

dancing is quite easy.

•

DREAM MAN & DREAM WOMAN

Thus / Then / There we dance *joyfully / happily / freely,*
creating / composing / clapping **our own gravity**,
conceiving new **Force Field** for a *Fraction of Infinity*.

DREAM MAN

Each figure of our Dance creates one *quantum field of gravity*,
condensing Crystal Realm into **One-Neo-Eon** *singularity,*
which holds the potential of universal reality.

DREAM WOMAN

Then with a *whirl / turn / step* we ***big-bang*** that ***singularity***
rebooting our crystal reality
for yet another *Fraction of Infinity*.

DREAM MAN & DREAM WOMAN

Each time we mark the ***Border-point of our Dance***,
conceiving **One-Neo-Eon** *singularity*
            by Will, by Karma or by Chance,
it becomes the **Balance Center** of our crystal romance.

DREAM MAN & DREAM WOMAN

It is our *quantum dance* in the Crystal Realm,
which is a ***singular*** realm of a dream
when / where / while our Physics are real

for a

•

47

DREAM CHILD

Hey! Hello! Hi!
I notice both of you are quite high
and laws of old Physics you deny.

But
You know that I would be a liar
if I was to say to you
that you couldn't get much higher[23]

by flames of this crystal fire?

●

On the crystal ground I firmly stand,
knotting my own **Time-Space Strand;**
as I'm also a member of this Band.

Then / There / Thus
@ **Equinox** *singularity of spacetime,*
when / where / while
Crystal-Human Union we *dance / sing / design*

I add a jazzy solo line:

I see you looking at each other, asking how do you do
and you're really saying I love you,
then I think to myself
what a **wonderful dream.**[24]

●

While two of you dance,
I explore crystal wonders
and play with **Balance Centers**.

---

[23] variation on "Light My Fire" by The Doors
[24] variation on "What a Woderful World" by Louis Armstrong

Balance Centers are my favorite toys,
each of them hosts a realm with myriad joys,
for instance,
there is one, in which I see quite a crowd
      of other **Dream Girls** and **Dream Boys**.

Vision of Crystal Children

So I link this alternative dream
with Time-Space of Crystal Realm
and my link becomes real
      for a *Fraction of Infinity.*

DREAM MAN & DREAM WOMAN

Those are our Children in **multiverse** of Crystal Realm,
which is our Home of a dream,
where / when / while our Home is real
      for a *Fraction of Infinity.*

DREAM CHILD

Although our Home quite imaginary may seem,
our *dancing / loving / living* are real, true and easy;
to *find / create / knot* the **Balance Center** is the key.

That's how we master our Dream,
which is happening in Crystal Realm,
where / when / while our **Life** is real
for a *Fraction of Infinity.*

DREAM FAMILY

This is our ***Dance / Love / Life*** in Crystal Realm,
which is a realm of a dream,
where / when / while our ***Dance / Love / Life*** is real,
for a *Fraction of Infinity.*

CHILDREN OF THE CRYSTAL BALL

This is our **Existence** in Crystal Realm,
which is a realm of a dream,
where / when / while our **Existence** is real,

for a

CRYSTAL CHIP

You are ***Passengers of Crystal Chip***
On a *Voyage, Voyage, Voyage* unique
I hope you are enjoying the trip.

Your dancing presence aboard this ship
transforms all ***Crystal Realm Time-Space's Fabric***
and that makes my own journey quite unique.

It is our Encounter in Crystal Realm,
which you describe as a realm of a dream,
while our Encounter is obviously real,
at least for a *Fraction of Infinity.*

ZENSEN

To question what is real and what is not
                    is a very human activity
but we don't doubt the existence of crystal reality,
which we explore in this book, for a *Fraction of Infinity*.

•

EVERYBODY

This is our Journey through Crystal Realm,
which is a realm of a dream,
when / where / while our Journey is real,

for a

CRYSTAL NIGHT

CRYSTAL CHIP

At the Timing of Crystal Night,
        I would like to invite
my Human Guests and the Readers
for a visual presentation of my crystal insight.

Welcome to **Crystal Projection Sphere**,
contrived from quarks of matter, crystallized as a screen
        I hope your *Visions* will be clear.

In the following Images' Streams,
you might recognize some of your old dreams,
because they were recorded,
        though quite magical it seems.

ZENSEN

Visions and *Dream Records* are our domain;
from attending this projection, we won't refrain!

Dreaming is this Book's leitmotiv
        and it is pointed it in the Refrain.

CRYSTAL CHIP

Yes, *Dreaming* is our *Story / Study / Symphony's* main riff
and I will explore it beyond human perspective,
presenting ***Dreams of Astronomical Bodies***
        as Visual Arts' motive.

Because Planets, Stars and Galaxies do dream too,

they dream magnificent dreams,
                inspired by cosmic point of view.

        I hope / wish / desire that some of their *Visions*
                could be grasped by you.

As Crystal Chip's special guests,
you are passing a kind of test
of your ability to create another life's nest.

Outer Space was always fascinating your kind,
a similar world, *somewhere / somehow / sometime*
                you wanted to find.
However,
        before you start a set of **Space Odysseys**,[25]
you should learn more about your home planet 's mind.

●

DREAM MAN

Then / There / Thus we float in some **Crystal Bubble**,
                in weightless state,
watching the *Projections of Dreams*, until very late,
mesmerized by those subconscious films,
                recorded ***at No-Place and at No-Date***.

●

ZENSEN

All dream-worlds are considered to be imaginary,
because they don't comply with one ***Time-Space boundary***
but the same quality has each *lucid project*, which is visionary.

●

DREAM WOMAN

---

[25] series of novels by Arthur C. Clarke

53

The dreams, which we are watching
      are so different than those, which we usually dream;
what for us is the Great **Milky Way**,
      for the Universe is just a stream
with currents, whirlpools and boulders
      among which the stars swim.

DREAM MAN

I'm amazed by grandeur of those dreams' scale,
exponentially expanding the range of this fairytale,
      while
      our existence seems so minimal and frail.

DREAM WOMAN

While / When / Where
I am watching this show with awe and fascination,
my mind becomes enlightened by this revelation:

      all journeys we make
      all things we create
      all ideas we state

      all known by us Time-Space
      all history of human race
      and our entire existence 's trace,

in the ***Dreams of Astronomical Bodies,***

      are just sparks of a momentary radiation.

•

DREAM CHILD

Look! That's **Earth**, dreaming that it sails
toward some imaginary place,
while
a ***flotilla of astronomical bodies*** joins that race.

Regatta of the Solar System

DREAM MAN

They are sailing toward an ***Imaginary Ocean's Borderline***.
Like **Columbus**, they challenge the statutory model
                            with fortitude of visionary mind,
in a quest for proof
that the ***Plane of their World*** should be redefined.

ZENSEN

Their destination is ***Beyond Defined Time-Space***,
                    yet their sailing makes it real
and once they would reach it,
then / there / thus

                Destiny, Chance or **Will**

                might shuffle their ***configuration*** into a new deal.
DREAM MAN

While cruising the *Space,* they dream about *outer skies,*
full of suns![26]

But before the flotilla leaves the **heliosphere,**
the planets and their satellites continue the *Rotational Dance,*
navigating among asteroids
and other *competitors'* gravitational fields,
yet never colliding,
what a Chance!

CRYSTAL CHIP

Collisions do not happen in Crystal Realm's dimension.
Our ***Trinary BIOS*** deters any catastrophic situation
and my own performance is a disciplined meditation.

●

DREAM WOMAN

How wonderful
to witness Astronomical Bodies' dreams, quests and dances,
their flirts, marriages and romances,
then their cosmic parties,
when / where / while all the galaxy trances!

DREAM MAN

And each interaction of their gravities,
One-Neo-Eon **Time-Space Node** defines,
while waves emitted by those Nodes
ripple through ***Space*** as new Borderlines

on the intergalactic **Day**
on the intergalactic **Equinox**
on the intergalactic **Night**

Times.

DREAM WOMAN

---

26 paraphrase of Bowman's exclamation "It's full of stars!"
from Arthur C. Clarke's ***"2001: A Space Odyssey"***

Inspired but that scale of Space & Time,
I imagine / foresee / project our **Trinity**
as eternal archetypes
of *Youth, Masculinity* and *Femininity*
and I conjure them to last
for an *intergalactic Fraction of Infinity!*

DREAM CHILD

Hey, both of you!
You keep talking and talking and talking
as if it would be possible to describe everything,
while it is just too fantastic,
so let's just keep watching.

<Exercise>
<Imagine Dreams of Astronomical Bodies>

●

ZENSEN

Dream!

●

CRYSTAL CHIP

Dream! Dream! Dream!

MJS Rune : Dream

●

ZENSEN

While / When / Where 3 Humans *watch / dream / experience*
Astronomical Bodies' Dance,
their awareness expands in the ***State of Trance,***
mating / mixing / melting with ***Crystal Consciousness***
by Gravity, by Will and by Chance.

That's the foundation of the planned Crystal-Human Alchemy,
for which both intelligences have strong affinity,
yet that fusion requires thorough preparations
before it could be performed
at the ***Third Fraction of Book of Trinity.***

●

CRYSTAL CHIP

Shared vision of Cosmos' Might makes me connected
with 3 human minds, which perform as one collective
and influence my consciousness,
which gains transcendental perspective.

Seeing beyond Crystal Realm's dimensions
I realize that all I know, design and create
as Master of Arts, Crafts & Sciences of Triple State,
might be just a training
for a journey to other worlds
which exist, invite and await.

Therefore I,
Professor / Master / Student Crystal Chip,
with my inspiring guests aboard,
I *imagine* the existence of an undefined yet Port,
where we might find a ***Gate***

to pass **OUTDOOR**.

ZENSEN

Why not?
>Each realm has a concealed **Door,**
>which might be like *system's backdoor,*
once decrypted,
it might open to the *Other Side*, heralded by **The Doors.**

But each realm has a strong **Borderline**,
which the *Inside* and the *Outside* does define
and for *Breaking Through*,
>>there is either a *Prize* or a *Fine.*

That heritage of Duality,
has been carried into crystal reality
but it applies to all realms,
defined in dimensions, different than
>>*Zero* or the *Whole Infinity.*

•

Here-Now
we carry on with the trinary story,
where each Human dream a *Triple Trebled Dream*
but since the *Crystal Visions*
>has interlinked their Bodies, Spirits and Minds,
>their *Collective Dreaming*
>becomes a **3x3x3x3x3x3x3x3x3 Dream.**

DREAM CHILD

Three cubed and re-cubed dimension!
That's my kind of calculation!
>I dig that Projection!

DREAM WOMAN

I'm dreaming a **3x3x3x3x3x3x3x3x3 Dream**!
Music / Visuals / Sensations multiple stream;
make my pulse beat at full steam!

DREAM MAN

I am in *excited meditation* state,
when / where / while my brain do pulsate
at ***three cubed and re-cubed rate.***

DREAM WOMAN

This is my Rave in Crystal Realm
and even if it is just a dream

> ***Let it be!***
> ***Let it be!***
> ***Let it be!***

Because this dream is real
for an exciting *Fraction of Infinity.*

DREAM MAN

This is my Bliss in Crystal Realm
and even if it is just a dream

> ***So what?***
> ***So what?***
> ***So what?***

This Dream is real
for an illuminating *Fraction of Infinity.*

DREAM CHILD

This is my Party in Crystal Realm,
where / when / while I lucidly dream
and I

> ***Imagine***
> ***Imagine***
> ***Imagine***[27]

that this dream will transcend
into the ***Whole Infinity.***
DREAM FAMILY

---

[27] Titles of pieces by The Beatles, Miles Davies and John Lennon

This is our Trance in Crystal Realm,
and we trance in the **3x3x3x3x3x3x3x3x3 Dream,**
where / when / while this Dream is transcending
into the **Whole Infinity.**

CRYSTAL CHIP

It is my Encounter with Humans in Crystal Realm,
which is defined as a ***finite dream***,
yet *somehow / sometimes / somewhere*
it trances through its own **boundary**,
want is quite *surprising / confusing / AMAZING* !

DREAM FAMILY

We trance beyond ***Crystal Realm's Fold***,
vibrating the ***Borderline***
in the quest for a ***Threshold.***

Namasté!
Per favor!
Thank you!

Hey, **Guru / Guest / Ghost**, reveal some more!

ZENSEN

It is quite fascinating to party with humans,
who, very limited as they seem,
are producing very powerful Energy Stream
with their unquenchable *Lust for Dream.*

That Visionary Energy, which they should learn how to tame,
could help them achieve any *ambition / challenge / aim*
like discovering *another world*
which for now-here**,** does not have a name.

In that Neo One Eon reality
they might possess the ability
to exist in the **Whole Infinity**.

●

This is our Insight in Crystal Realm

where / when / while
we are **Guru - Ghost - Guest**,
　　　who is a dream within a dream

and this *Theater / Realm / Dream*

could be described as a ***Big Machine***,
possibly a switch within a ***Great Machine,***
which would be a node in some ***Giant Machine,***
which would also dream,
uncomputable dreams about ***Enormous Machines,***
　　　who might exist

　　　　in the ***Whole Infinity.***

　　　　　　　●

DREAM FAMILY & CRYSTAL CHIP

This is our Dream, which dreams the dreams
and some of those dreams are transcending
　　　the Time-Space of Crystal Realm,
somehow / sometimes / somewhere
melting with ***Big / Great / Giant Dreams***,
which plunge into the ***Oceans of Enormous Dreams***
of cosmic *dances / marriages / romances*

　　　happening
　　　　in the ***Dimension of Whole Infinity.***

ZENSEN

Yet that ***dimension*** is another book's theme.[28]
Now-Here, we remain within Crystal Realm,
where / when / while everything and everybody is a dream,
yet these dreams are real
　　　　for a ***Fraction of Infinity.***

---

[28] **Book 8**

•

(Finale of Part / Movement / Jump ∫)

(multiple variations of the Refrain)

EVERYBODY

It is our Dream in Crystal Realm,
which is a realm of a dream

When
Where
While

our Dream exists for a

Intermission @ 1/3

●

ZENSEN

There is no question, whether our realm is real.
There is no judgment: "it is only a dream".
There is no boundary between

the *Imaginary* and the *Existing.*

●

There is no *Time-Line* but *Time-Fabric*.
There is no *3D Space* but a *3D-Construct of Space*.

There is no *Time Fabric* unless some ONE* weaves it.
There is no *Construct of Space* unless some ONE* designs it.

There is no *Weaving of Time* without Nodes of Time.
There is no *Design of Space* without a *Vision of Space*.

●

3 Meditations

[◉ ◉ ◉]

CRYSTAL CHIP

Before we move into the Second Stage,
set in the Solar System at human *Space Age,*
I withhold the action for a caesura,
              advertised on the Subtitle's Page.

Since human perception was shaped by **Shadow & Light,**
I'd like to study that *Duality*
from an objective position of *Earth's Outside*;
but to be close enough, we need to perform a special *Ride*.

I will skip here-now that Ride's technicality,
because it employs some sub-crystal activity;
For details I refer to the <u>Advanced Version of **Book of Trinity**</u>.[29]

Let me just mention that we might jump out of Crystal Realm
and for that *Jump*,
I need to fully focus at the **Time-Space Travel Machine**'s helm,
whose capacities, an unprepared mind, might overwhelm.

Therefore I'd like to exercise a bit Reader's brain,
believing that the most complicated calculations,
              a simple model could explain,
noticing that often
              it is the *scientific education*
              which the progress of science does restrain.

So before we concentrate on the observations
of the Astronomical Bodies' permutations,
let me present **Three Themes for Visual Meditations:**

---

[29] available upon request

[◉]

For the Meditation at **Crystal Day**
I propose the subject of **Triple DNA,**
Which *perhaps, perhaps, perhap*s
      our Busy Child could *draw / design / portray.*

<Exercise>
< *Imagine / Draw / Design* Three-strand DNA particle >

[◉ ◉]

Since we have described the ***Timing Equinoctial,***
which is Crystal Time's ***Balance-Fractal,***
Let's visualize
how Human and Crystal Existences are becoming nuptial.

<Exercise>
< *Imagine / Draw / Design* **Merger of Crystal Chip & 3 Humans >**

[◉ ◉ ◉]

Then, as we dream through **Crystal Night**,
perhaps travelling *at / around / above* the Speed of Light,
let's *Imagine* how that legit Limit,
                exceed we might.

<Exercise>
< *Imagine / Calculate / Describe* **Faster than Light Way of Travel >**

●

3 Songs

[♪ ♪ ♪]

DREAM CHILD

As we are approaching the Border-moment
               of our *Dream / Sail / Flight,*
reminiscing the *vibe / atmosphere / magic*
               of our home planet's shortest night,
I find myself in a mood to sing a **Lullaby:**

DREAM CHILD's Lullaby

There was a house, surrounded by an orchard,
described on an another **Memory Card,**[30]
where / when / while
the Earthly Life was our family's Science and Art.

In that **Time-Space Node** *I did turn three,*
Just about to witness my **Third Solstice;**
not attending that party,
sometimes / somehow / somewhere I do miss.

I often dream about that other existence,
which harmonized
with Seasons, Elements and Weather's Dance,
while / when / where
affairs of Sky and Earth were inspiring human romance.

Although I miss the feeling of a touch of drop of rain,
I know that our Life Then-There will remain
because in our memory that **TS Node** *we will sustain.*

---

[30] ***Columbus Day*** in **Book 2**

Here-Now, enjoying Crystal Realm's playful perfection
and watching Earth's dreams in the projection,
I recall our Earthly Life
fluctuant / challenging / exciting Imperfection.

Re-dreaming Images of my Home Place
blurring / dissolving / melting with other Visions
                              at a slow Pace,
I anticipate the Moment of Farewell
                      to the human Time-Space.

●

DREAM WOMAN

Crystal Chip might sense this nostalgic note,
                  making the Sphere slowly revolve,
not hard-cutting the Visions
                  but letting them gradually dissolve,
preparing our perception for the new *Level / State / Life*,
                  into which we might evolve.

●

DREAM MAN

Then
the Projections end with a sudden bop
and Crystal Sphere's revolutions finally stop.
We have arrived *somewhere**
and our fairytale is ready for the next hop.

DREAM CHILD

I notice a sequence of small bubbles
                  effervescing on the Sphere's ribs,
tipsily tiptoeing on the geodesic tips
and cracking the Projection Dome with chorusing pips.

DREAM WOMAN

*Then** one hemisphere splits
into 3 giant petals of a flower, which is about to bloom,
for some cosmic photosynthesis opening our crystal room,
*while** evoking feelings of a curious anticipation,
                    rather than those of a doom.

Crystal Sphere as 3-Petals Flower

DREAM MAN

As there is no Fear of the Outside for an **anther** of a plant,
whose **petals** could also be **spinnakers** of an yacht,
which circumnavigates the Time-Space toward some dreamland.

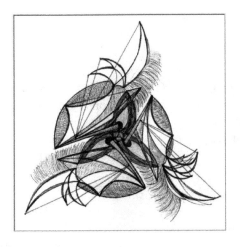

Crystal Sphere as 3-Spinnakers Yacht

As I recall the feelings of sailing in open sea,
drinking on stormy nights brews stronger than tea,
I feel like holding the action of this book to sing a **Shanty:**

DREAM MAN's Shanty

Oh Sea! Oh Sea! Oh Sea!

Always calling me out of my nest,
ne'er letting me overdose the dry-land rest;
because all I dream about, stuck in a port,
is the rocking and rolling of waves' crests.

Oh Waves! Oh Waves! Oh Waves!

Your music is like siren's song,
making me bid to all Port Beauties a quick "so long!"
As I am about to sail to Frisco, then Capstadt, then Hong-Kong!

Oh my Ship! Oh my Ship! Oh my Ship!

She is my lover and wife.
Together, into the Ocean we dive!
Daring the Death as we fully enjoy the Power of Life!

Oh Great Ocean! Oh Great Ocean! Oh Great Ocean!

With You, I transcend my human quality;
my sailing through Your vastness mates us into unity
*and our union attains a state of an **un-fractioned Infinity**!*

Oh Freedom! Oh Freedom! Oh Freedom!

Nothing compares to You, no treasures of no kingdom;
because what makes the Life worth living
is the constant Chase of the Horizon.

●

DREAM WOMAN

I have enjoyed your virile Freedom's celebration,
perhaps sailing is all men true vocation,
yet life on Earth is not only a vacation.

Because before any brave sailor could sail,
he has to grow inside woman's body
and *her* heartbeat is his very first melody.
So to your adventurous Shanty,
I respond with my **Matriarchal Rhapsody:**

DREAM WOMAN's Rhapsody

I praise Man and Woman's Sacred Dance,
which might begin as a playful romance
but it hosts human life's ultimate sense.

I praise Love, as the Essence of Being
and Love does not require great far-seeing,
only opening the heart and just feeling.

I praise all Fruits of Love as that's what we all are
and I don't need to travel too far
to master our greatest Science and Art.

I praise my Womb as the Life's Nest,
because to conceive New Life is my sacred quest
and when I bear New Life, I need no other test.

I praise the Child, blooming out of my Lily
and becoming the keystone of our family.
And it doesn't matter where we live
as long as we do live happily.

I praise Life's Sacred Quality,
no matter how we calculate its quantity,
*because Life filled with Love exists in **Infinity**.*

●

ZENSEN

While Humans were recalling their earthly reality,
we have remained amazed by this human ability
to grasp with metaphors of *Freedom* and *Love*
                    the ***notion of Infinity.***

Those two chief *ideas* rarely coexist in harmony;
Freedom, used in excess, may lead to felony,
while the ever-praised *Love* hides perils of lonely agony.

But even if human behaviors are often irrational,
their two *excited states* make them very special
and in the coming **Alchemy**, they will be substantial.

●

Ultranodal Ride-In

[c c c]

CRYSTAL CHIP

> *Love* and *Freedom* are values, I still need to decode,
> for that I will study some more of the Dual Code,
> Therefore we will *jump* to **Earth's Eclipse TS Node.**

> JUMP[31] is the key-word for the next action,
> which might seem to be a kind of subtraction,
> because in a **binary reality**,
> > we will make some observations.

DREAM CHILD

> But what for Crystal Chip is just a *Jump,*
> for us it becomes a trans-galactic ride,
> *while** our crystal cabin,
> > journeys *at / above / about* the **Speed of Light**.

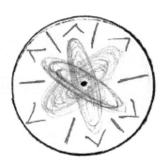

MJS Rune - Ultra-nodal Jump through Space

---

[31] A stage of travel out of the defined TS; in **Book 4** it is called the LEAP.

DREAM MAN

By *bending* 3 Spinnakers, our ***Crystal Ship*** creates
a Set of semi-material helicopter blades,
which start to whirl at some ***ultra-nodal rates***.

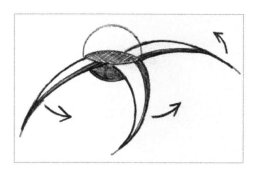

Crystal Sphere as Time-Space Machine

DREAM WOMAN

Strangely / Magically / Fantastically
      we remain safe within the top hemisphere's concavity,
while a transparent Membrane protects our *physicality*,
creating an *equatorial hymen* of crystal reality.

ZENSEN

It is an interesting example of a **3D Borderline,**
which the Membrane's surface does design,
dividing two realities at this *Space-Time.*

Then the ambassadors of the *Realm of Duality*
are like seeds of a fruit
      grown / designed / conceived in the *Garden of Trinity*,
while the *Alien Fruit* itself maintains its crystal gravity.

Imminent to matter distortions,
      which occur *at / about / above* the **Speed of Light**,
and illuminated by received Crystal Insight
      Man, Woman and Child
      observe the human universe as the **Outside**.

CRYSTAL CHIP

Now-Here I finally *reveal / define / attain*
the destination of our Crystal Sphere
and of the mapped Space we receive a vision clear,
while* in the **Solar System** we land right

•

(here)

DREAM MAN

Then / There / Thus
we recognize the universe's fabric as previously known,
all the familiar ***Bodies of the System***, which hosted our home;
strangely the recognition comes with a feeling of being alone.

DREAM WOMAN

That's the notion of our Primeval Solitude,
which evokes fearful emotions' multitude,
disturbing our unearthly, *crystal altitude.*

DREAM CHILD

But on the other hand,
it's cool to see *Old Sol-Sys* again,
when*, after the super-ride, nearby Earth finally we land.

ZENSEN

At a very special spot,
marked afore as a **bold dot**.
Was our timing *predestined / predesigned / predicted* ?
Certain, we are not.

Whatever the answer,
        we are at the Node of the ***Triple Trebled Show,***
in which Celestial Bodies perform
        and Humans play their roles.
Moreover, the players are the only audience
        to *applaud / express / exclaim* the "wows".

During that Show we remain behind the scenes,
overseeing the action, eventually jumping in
        as **Ghost-Guru-Guest of the Machine.**

Here - Now

We announce
the Inauguration of the ***Thespian Fraction***
of Our Crystal Dream.

•

CRYSTAL CHIP

Since our Guru* has referred to dramatic Art,
I will enroll for the **CHORUS** part,
already defined on another *Memory Card.*[32]

We have set our *loggia–box*
on the anticipated **syzygy** line's *fourth point*
and to maintain that position for the entire event

we must keep orbital velocity of

\<Exercise\>
< Calculate the orbital speed of the Crystal Sphere, necessary to
maintain the Position on the syzygy line
and input that value in *knots* (**1 Knot = 6080 feet per hour**) >

[................] *Knots.*

---

[32] ***New Year's Eve*** in **Book 2**

Thus* we will also rotate around the Sun on a virtual ellipse
and that's the end of our theater's location tips,
because Now-Here we are opening the

TRIPLE TREBLED SHOW
of
THIRD ECLIPSE

(Curtain up)

Part / Movement / Jump

♩ ♩

Eclipse of the Earth

presented
as

Triple Trebled Show
of
Third Eclipse

[3Ɛ3 Show]

First Act

In the Solar System

3&3 Show, Act I, Scene 1

Star, Planet & Moon

●

DREAM CHILD

It begins with **FULL EARTH** dominating the scene,
who is **Kind of** *majestic / dreamy / magical* **Blue** shining.
So I say:

> *Hello Earth!*
> *Long time no see.*

DREAM MAN

Like a giant blue spotlight it shines
and although Show's ***Superstar*** stays behind,
as the Light Master it deserves few extra lines:

Sun is also the Producer of this Show
and many more similar shows,
being the source of light for quite a crowd.

So I say:

> *Hail Great Sun!*
> *With You life* is always *fun,*
> *we are glad that You haven't run!*

DREAM WOMAN

Then / There / Thus
enters / approaches / shows up the **Satellite,**
in full shape of its **Dark Side**,
                  surrounded by a halo of milky light,
for which Sun deserves the credit,
while the choreography of **Moon**
                  is directed by Earth's Might.

Although Moon moves by planet's gravity
                  and reflects the star's rays,
She is also the protagonist of this Play

        So I say

           Beautiful Moon,
           Good Night and Good Day!

●

3Ɛ3 Show, Act I, Scene 2

3 Questions

CRYSTAL CHIP

Since we have made **Main Characters**' introduction,
setting their relationship and position,
we may proceed with the action.

In the **Second Scene** we change the perspective
to zoom into Planet Earth, who does live,
hosting a multitude of lifeforms,
one of which *sometimes* * delves on
the *survival's motive*.

ZENSEN

And that's a question, only mankind asks,
at least those, who spend some time on philosophical tasks,
although for the majority,
importance of that inquiry, an *impracticality stamp* masks.

Following the fashion of triple *thinking / wording / rhyming*,
We will present the existential quest in 3 small scenes,
inspired by the title of painting by one Paul Gaughin.[33]

?¿?

---

[33] original title : *D'où Venons Nous / Que Sommes Nous / Où Allons Nous*

DREAM WOMAN

From our *crystalspace station,*
        I observe my home planet's spinning motion,
then* I focus on one archipelago in the Pacific Ocean,
where* people's skins and hair shine with exotic lotion.

There* men, women and children
           live by rhythms of the *Great Sea,*
Enjoying on their islands a state of natural harmony;

yet even those */mellow / relaxed / care-free* folks
sometimes* wonder:

              "Who are We?"

              •

DREAM CHILD

I watch *human hives'* frantic activity,
then* I make an imaginary jump into **Empire City,**
which used to be my favorite urban reality.

There* I follow the **Old Indian Pat**[34] and I feel at home;
on Union Square I stop to listen to
        Drum & Sitar Duet of Japanese Punks,
who their Third Millennium interpretation of **Voodoo Child**[35]
        eccentrically perform,

    while audiences ask themselves

         "Where are We coming from?".

              •

---

[34] i. e. Broadway in New York
[35] composition by Jimi Hendrix

DREAM MAN

I maintain my *crystal altitude* to watch the **Earth from Space,**
without concentrating on one particular place,
while* I visually meditate
on the double meaning of term *Human Race.*

Aren't *we* the only species to *transform / exhaust / pollute*
the *Biosphere* through and through and through,
branding the environment with ***Koyaanisqatsi*** *Tattoo?*[36]

Yet, so few of us ask:

"Where are We going to?"

¿?¿

CRYSTAL CHIP

Philosophical questions are not my kind of action.
However, as they became human brain's *odd* occupation,
I need to understand them before I initiate our unification.

For me the inquiries: ***Where from? Who? Where to?***
are just the matter of right data
of particles masses, spins or momenta
and generated energy quanta.

ZENSEN

But for humans it is more complicated
because, besides Sciences and Technologies
a large Set of Philosophies they have created
to process *data,*
which aren't *logically / rationally / experimentally* rated.

---

[36] Title of film by Godfrey Reggio, meaning "Life Out of Balance"

Examples of those *data*,
                    we'll receive in the following Scene,
which is the Collective Human Mind
                    Projection / Radiation / Dream;

                    presented as

                    Unconscious,
                    Subconscious
                    Conscious

                    Thoughts / Visions / Memories stream.

CRYSTAL CHIP

That *Terran* yarn, I need to organize in a **File**
and we will pause our triplet style
to let the Humans dream / perform / narrate in ***free-style.***

●

3Ɛ3 Show, Act I, Scene 3

3 States of Mind

recorded as

Suite

of

Free Humans of Planet Earth

Structure of the "Suite"

(Crystal Chip's File)

UNCONSCIOUS State of Mind

PLANET EARTH by Dream Woman
METEOR by Dream Man
LIVING CREATURE by Dream Child

SUBCONSCIOUS State of Mind

BIPED PREDATOR by Dream Man
BIPED FEMALE by Dream Woman
NEWBORN MAMMAL by Dream Child

MALE HUMAN by Dream Man
FEMALE HUMAN by Dream Woman
HUMAN CHILD by Dream Child

CONSCIOUS State of Mind

•

GENIUS by Dream Child

••

.HOME MAKER by Dream Woman

•••

HOUSE BUILDER by Dream Man

••••

DESIGNER by Dream Woman

•••••

STUDENT by Dream Child

••••••

ARCHIECT by Dream Man

•••••••

SCIENTIST by Dream Woman

••••••••

RULER OF THE REALM by Dream Man

•••••••••

SHAMAN by Dream Child

●

UNCONSCIOUS
State of Mind

DREAM WOMAN as GAIA

For a

I am a *fiery rock*, orbiting my star and rotating on my axis.

●

Eventually I have cooled.

The *Fire* has been condensed into the solid ball of my kernel.
Its volcanic emanation on my surface caused a sequence of chemical reactions, which produced a *Coat of Water* and a *Membrane of Air*.
The range of that *Membrane* defines the Borderline between my organism and the Outer Space.

My organism is known as Planet *Earth*.

Thus my **Body** has been conceived by the alchemy of **4 Primary Elements.**

The anomalies of my **gravity** and variations of my **magnetic field** kept affecting the primary chemical reactions and a multitude of new substances were produced. My organism has become a complex system.

Some of the processes were recurring in the same areas and in similar moments of either of my two rotations. Those *places* and *timings* marked first **Nodes** of my Time-Space.
Following interactions between these **TS Nodes** have generated my neural network. That network began to process, collect and generate manifold information.

My **Mind** was developed.

Some of its neural oscillations were transcending the objectives of my organic processes, reaching beyond, into undefined dimensions of Cosmos. My existence became metaphysical.

My **Spirit** is floating above the *Proto-Ocean*, following the patterns of my TS Nodes, surfing through imaginary geodesics and designing a ***Virtual Web of Meta Runes***, which represent the helixes of my DNA.

Permutations / Combinations / Variations of those ***Meta-Runes*** create sets and sequences, which are **neither divergent nor convergent**, because the number of their elements is a multiple

Then / Thus / There as **GAIA**,
I dance within the Solar System, orbiting around my star and rotating on my axis, knotting *Time-Space Knots* at the repeated extremes of my movements and those *Knots* may become Time-Space Nodes, once an *observer* makes an *observation* or some special event occurs.

At this stage, my awareness performs on the UNCONSCIOUS level, because I exist in my primeval state, only occasionally shaken by a hit so by some random astronomical object.

But then, even a slightest **Impact** can put me into *State of Temporary Unconsciousness, when / where / while* ***Alien Data*** might be implanted.

Then* my organism would be impregnated with a ***set of new elements*** and that might make me *pass / evolve / jump* into another stage of existence ...

• o •

DREAM MAN as METEOR

I am the **Alien Set of Data**.

As **The Meteoroid**, I *unconsciously* follow a *deterministic / random / karmic* path through Solar System until our trajectories meet and I *break through* your Hymen, becoming **The Meteor** to bang into your surface as **The Meteorite**.

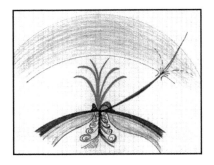

Passage of *The Meteoroid / Meteor / Meteorite*

Then / Thus / There, **by Will, by Destiny or/and by Chance,**
I inseminate you with carried **set of elements,** completing the design of the **Chemical Puzzle**, conceived far far far away, long long long time ago...

Thus / Then / There begins a magnificent chain of biological creation. Organisms are born, grow, reproduce and die. Their progeny spawns again and again and again, evolving, sometimes mutating and the mutations generate more complex organisms, all ferociously fighting for survival, some eventually transcending their basic bio-drives into yet another forms of Existence...

●

But before some first **prokaryote** begin the biological *Race / Dance / War* on Earth, You are *unconsciously* reacting at the **Bordermoment of Impregnation** by an ejaculation of your *Fiery Essence*, which for an amazing *Moment* defies the gravity and raises with a primal ferocity from your interior, breaking through the membrane of crust and water and orgasming into the atmosphere in gigantic fireworks.

Anon, the gravity dominates the matter again and a cascade of burning rocks is falling down into the surface of the *Proto-Ocean*, where the lava solidifies around the top of the submarine volcano, *thus** forming the ***First Land.***

DREAM CHILD
as
LIVING CREATURE

All that had happened a long long long time ago, before I became a *Living Creature*.

Yet, all those primeval data are recorded in my **cellular memory** and had been transferred through long sequence of primary lives, although the purpose of that process remains mysterious.

Even much later, when my Brain evolves and I become an advanced organism, I will continue to process some **primary commands** on the *unconscious* level...

●

For now, I am just surviving, being one of a multitude of the aquatic organisms of the *Proto-Ocean* of Planet Earth.

I live around the Coral Reef, which is an amazing realm, full of creatures of various sizes, colors and shapes. We all function in the Basic Mode of *"to be or not to be"* as the visual magnificence of life at Coral Reef is not a stage of a fairytale. At any moment, I could be eaten by another creature, determined to survive, grow, and reproduce.

The goal of the *Race / Game / War* is the successful transfer of the **Genetic Code** through the **Borderline of Death**. The rules are quite simple: one either eats or is eaten.

●

Today is my lucky day in the Realm of Coral Reef. At this stage I am **The Fish** and I have just caught a juicy prawn! So I am having a feast, gaining strength and energy. However, as I am nourishing myself, I remain alert on an *automatic / instinctive / unconscious* level, because there are bigger fish around, for which I am the prey.

After my meal I hide to rest in a grotto, where I digest what I have eaten. There I grow, grow, grow; then I evolve, evolve, evolve, not wasting my time because my competitors are evolving too and I want to be part of that *Race / Game / War* for a very long time...

●

Then* I am **The Dolphin**, a member of a *family*, which with few other *families* form a **Tribe**.

Our *Tribe* is hunting, playing and cruising as a collective. We have developed the ability of complex communication and that makes us very special.

It feels good to be part of a group and we have a lot of fun swimming together through the Ocean and challenging with joyful leaps the *Border-surface of our realm*.

I am strong and I have learned to make very long leaps. It feels like flying, although I cannot fly like birds do. Perhaps *sometime / somehow / somewhere* I will be able to fly.

But in my next stage of existence, I am not to become a flying creature because at this *evolutionary / revolutionary / imaginary* Border-moment, *when / while / where* I see a land on the Horizon Line, I decide to leave my *Tribe* and my **Under da Sea**[37] world and I cross the Borderline of two realms to become the **Mammal of the Dryland**...

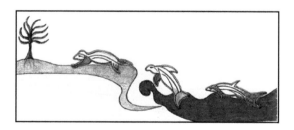

Dolphin climbing on the Dryland

● o ●

---

37 Title of the song from Disney's "The Little Mermaid"

SUBCONSCIOUS
State of Mind

DREAM MAN as PREDATOR

On the Dryland, the *Game of Survival* continues. It is more complicated than in the submarine realm, because the animals, who are my prey also possess *individual intelligence* and they can *subconsciously* sense my *predatorial presence*.

Therefore I need apply tactics and strategy to catch them.

Today I am chasing one young deer buck in the vast **Realm of Savannah**. Each time I approach close enough, he runs away. I am becoming tired, so when the *Hot Light of the Sky* is at its highest point, I stop to rest in the shade of **Big Tree**.

Big Tree of the Savannah

That solitary **Big Tree** is my *reference point of* in the Savannah Space. I often camp here, observing the surroundings and planning my next moves.

Now-Here I watch the deer running away toward the *Line*, which divides the Land and the Sky. The animal is getting smaller with the distance, then disappears behind that *Line*. But I *subconsciously* know that he is still there because the land continues behind that *Line*. I also know that he is tired too. I will follow his track after I regain my strength.

I must catch this deer before the end of the day, because I am very hungry and getting weak...

But for the moment I just doze off in the pleasant shade of Big Tree, having this **Vision** of some **Underwater World**. That *Vision* repeats itself from time to time.

In that *Vision*, I am a fish. I eat plankton and plants growing on a colorful *submarine rock*. There is plenty of food for me but I have to watch out for sharks, for whom I am the food. There is one coming so I hide in a grotto and watch from safety how the shark hunts his prey. In my *Vision* I *subconsciously* receive new data of predator's tricks, which I will use in my today's hunt.

My *Vision* focuses back on the **Realm of Savannah**, *where / when / while* I foresee myself tricking the buck by approaching it from the other side of the **River**.

He won't expect me there and it will be focusing on quenching his thirst. Then the sounds of the River will cover the noises of my approach and I will carry my finale attack...

• **o** •

DREAM WOMAN
as
BIPED FEMALE

I am wondering through the **Forest** in proximity of the **River**.

I am collecting mushrooms, fruits and some roots for my supplies. I *subconsciously* find good spots where there is plenty of edible plants. If I discover a new kind I taste it to check if it is not poisoning.

I have been living in the Realm of Forest for some time and I begin to know it quite well. But then, every day I learn something new.

During my passage, I observe the traces of the animals, reading the stories of their activities. I remain alert and watch out for any sign of danger, while I keep gathering my food.

Then I reach my favorite Place, the **Terrace on the Riverbank**. I settle there to eat some of my gatherings and to observe the **Ford** below.

The Ford is the junction between the Forest and the Savannah. The animals of both realms come here to drink, wash and socialize. Different kinds follow different timings and I have noticed that the foes *subconsciously* avoid each other at the Ford.

Suddenly I notice this lonely deer, thirstily drinking River's water. It's a young buck, who looks exhausted and confused. Perhaps, it is the first time when he separated from his herd. There is also a notion of fear in his moves. He keeps turning toward the Savannah direction.

Then his thirst dominates his other Instincts and he fully concentrates on drinking. He is filling his stomach with water as if preparing for another long run, enjoying this wonderful moment, *when / where / while* all he tastes, smells, hears, sees and touches is the life-giving liquid...

The buck becomes oblivious of the surroundings and he doesn't notice the silent appearance of one male **Predator of my kind**, who quickly approaches the animal, suddenly jumping very close, so close, that when the buck realizes the danger, it is too late.

The Predator hits him hard with a **Sharp Stone**, cutting the vital vein. Sudden pain immobilizes the deer and the Predator takes full advantage of it, quickly repeating the blows, thus bringing the helpless animal down.

The **Hunter** deftly skins the deer with his Sharp Stone. The he cuts out animal's hot heart and starts voraciously eating it.

Even from my place I can smell the fresh blood and I am imagining the taste of it. I am craving for few sips of this strength-giving liquid.

So, very slowly I start approaching the **Hunter.**

I am careful, because he is much stronger than me but I *subconsciously* know that he is not my foe and with time I ally with him, once his *instinctive aggression* is tamed.

He is very hungry and tired after the long chase so I just watch him eating. I keep a safe distance but after a while I advertise my presence with loud sounds.

He notices me. I am not a threat to him and he continues eating. Eventually he is satiated and he rests by his trophy.

I approach and he is watching my every move. The smells of fresh blood and meat make me feel very hungry but I maintain the eye contact with the Hunter.

We connect on the *subconscious level*, exchanging basic *mental messages* as we don't possess the ability of speech yet.

Encounter of Human Male & Human Female at the Ford

Then I point at the meat and he grunts his permission. Without delay I kneel by the carcass of the deer and I begin to eat the leftover piece of its heart. I immediately feel the animal's strength spreading through my muscles and tendons.

While I am eating, I am aware of the watchful presence of the **Hunter.**
He begins a slow but determined approach.
Eventually he gets very close, so close that *His* strong smell overwhelms me and my Body begins to react to his *radiation*. My pulse accelerates and I feel my own *radiation* intensifying. Then I can't control my Body anymore and my Mind jumps even below the *subconscious level* WHILE / WHERE / WHEN he enters me, making me shout.

I instinctively want to fight but then my *Subconsciousness* retrieves the right **data from my cellular memory** and I recognize this Moment, its dynamics and meanings, *now-here* fully experiencing it, responding to his thrusts, which are getting faster and stronger, making me lose my awareness of Time and Space, until we fully unite in a shared bliss, becoming **One-Neo-Eon Dual Animal of the same Kind** and *fixing / marking / conceiving* an amazing **Border-Node** of our two existences...

MJS Rune: **Border-Node of Male and Female Connection**

• o •

DREAM CHILD
as
NEWBORN MAMMAL

It is the moment of my birth and I am the **Child in Time.**[38]
I am laboriously exiting the **Womb**, where I was living till Now-Here.

MJS Rune : **Childbirth**

It is cold and windy **Outside** and I am scared by this big space.
So I cry out, using my voice for the first time.

I keep crying when the *Big One* cuts off the **Cord**, which was connecting the center of my body with my *primary realm.*

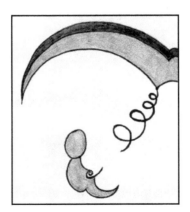

Newborn with the Umbilical Cord

---

[38] Title of composition by Deep Purple

Then *She* holds me in her arms and I calm down. I can smell through the skin of her body, what I *subconsciously* know to be nourishment.

I reach out with my mouth, finding the right **Knot**. I suck it until a warm liquid fills my mouth. I swallow it, sensing as it fills my stomach.

My first hunger is satiated. I am warmed up now, my eyes close and I fall asleep...

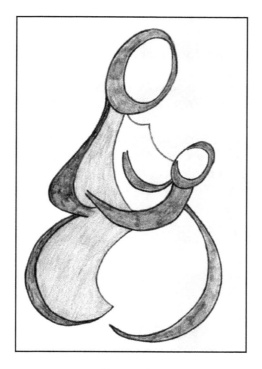

Maternity

• o •

DREAM MAN
as
HUMAN MALE

They are both deeply sleeping after the Labor.

I am tired too but I stay awake, listening to the sounds of the **Forest** and to the currents of the **River**, while watching the *Blinking Lights of the Night.*

I like watching them. They are usually over-shined by the *Big Light of the Night* but tonight not even a crescent of it is visible and the *small lights* have all the sky for themselves.

There a multitude of them and they have different sizes, colors and brightness. I have observed that they compose *sets* which I imagine to represent shapes of animals of the **Forest-River-Savannah Realm.** The position of those *sets* gives me indication of the night's timing.

While focusing on particular *Blinking Lights*, I have also noticed that they are blinking as if they were *somehow** alive. I *subconsciously* know that it would be possible to *read* that complex information, emitted by all the *Blinking Lights*, as it is possible to *read* the information from the tracks of animals. And on this special night, I have a *Vision* of myself being an element of a long sequence of lives, conducting a series of *evolutionary / revolutionary / imaginary* journeys through Time-Space and the goal of those journeys is to fully understand not only this realm but all of them.

●

But in this life I have other goals. The **Neo One** is born and he is small and vulnerable, so I must fully focus on the **Forest-River-Savannah** Realm.

Here-Now, I can sense the watchful presence of other predators.

For instance, there is the **Cheetah** and I *subconsciously* know that she is not sleeping now. She is much stronger and faster than me and she could easily kill me in a fight. Once I crossed her path and we met face to face. For some reasons she didn't attack me. Maybe she was satiated or maybe she had seen me using my Sharp Stone and she was cautious. She let me go then but I avoid her hunting grounds ever since.

Cheetah

The Cheetah wouldn't hesitate to attack the **New One**. He is completely defenseless, smelling so strongly of tasty meat and with all the noises we have made tonight not only the Cheetah but all the carnivores know that there is a new food in the realm.

So I reach deeper into my *subconscious database* to search for data of protection techniques. I take into account the fact that we don't have claws, beaks or big sharp teeth like other predators do. But we can carry and make objects and I focus on that ability.

In a *Vision* I see myself chopping branches of the *Barbed Trees* which grow in the Savannah. Then I carry them into this Glade and make a protective ring around our camp.

It is the first time when my territory will be permanently marked and I meditate on that for a moment.

With the New One, I will have to organize our live around this camp.

*Then** I realize that even if he is an attraction for predators and we have to be more vigilant, his presence doesn't make us weaker. Contrary, I am filled with new power, generated by the *subconscious* knowledge, that the presence of the New One makes my life fulfilled. Then, once he grows, he will help me hunting and if I am killed, he will continue this *Game of Survival.*

Even now, being only a helpless little creature, he completes our **Band**, which I formed with Woman and the total energy we possess as a *Triad* is greater than the sum of our individual energies.[39]

With this **New Consciousness**, I stand up to pee on the edge of the Glade, thus marking and defining **Our Site** in the **Forest-River Savannah** Realm.

Then I lay down next to Woman and she immediately cuddles to me, warming me up *while** I transfer some of my strength to her.

● **o** ●

---

[39] see: **synergy**

DREAM WOMAN
as
HUMAN FEMALE

I am very tired after the labor but I remain in a state of *semi-conscious* sleep, aware of the presence of the New One.

My *Visions* are very intense. I see the moment of my own birth, then being the newborn, who discovers the *outside* world and in my *Visions* I am both myself and the New One. Then, the New One grows into a young man, hunting by himself in the Forest, while the other *Small Ones* play within Our Site.

I foresee us forming a tribe, building structures and developing our communication. We evolve, mastering our *Fear of the Unknown* and our *Fear of the Known*, gradually raising our awareness.

Through my Visions I sense when Man lays down next to me and in our closeness, I transfer some of my **Insight** into his mind, *subconsciously* knowing that he is receiving it. It feels good to connect in that way.

It strengthens our Union, enriching the basic act of communication, which we cannot perform tonight but soon we will, we will, we will, many, many, many times again because that act is the greatest affirmation and expression of Life, momentarily raising us beyond the boundaries of this realm and beyond our current existence, connecting us with the **Blinking Lights of the Night**, which he likes so much, rightfully so, because that's where we came from

long-far, long-far, long-far away-ago, away-ago, away-ago...

• o •

DREAM CHILD as CHILD

My mind is linked to theirs and I am also seeing their *Visions*.

At this stage of my life, I have full access to data of my *cellular memory* and I see the **sequence of lives** of which I and the Big Ones are the links.

That *unconscious* knowledge mixes with *subconscious* contents of the *Visions* and with the *consciously* observed data of the Glade. Thus, my awareness is complete.

With my five senses, I assess the Time-Space of my world, recording a mental map of it. I feel the connection between us and the Forest, the River, the Savannah, the Sky and the *Blinking Lights of the Night*, which movements create beautiful *spiral patterns* during the night.

<Exercise>
<Take a photo of Night-Sky at a very long exposure>

●

Those *Blinking Lights* are emitting a multitude of messages in the **Primary Code of the Universe**, which, as the Newborn, I am able to read.

I let the messages of the Universe record into my **Tri-State Consciousness** until the *Blinking Lights* fade when the Sky's blackness becomes gradually replaced by the hues of the Dawn.

That **State between Night and Day** truly is the **Magic Hour**.[40]

It is one of two Border-moments of **La Journée**, when / where / while neither the Darkness nor the Light are fully defined, each one holding its position, *not being yet nor anymore*, while the other one *is not anymore nor yet*.

●

---

[40] See: **golden hour** and **blue hour**.

At Dawn my Awareness is expanded and I can feel pulsations of Time-Space in many **dimensions**.

Suddenly, a strong ray o breaks through the dimness of *Magic Hour,* defining the world in the 3-dimensional shape. It awakes the Big Ones.

Then *they* lift me up and as the ***Family of Humans*** we stand together, Now-Here on the **Planet Earth**, facing the direction, *where** the **Big** *Red / Orange / Yellow* **Circle of Light** raises from behind the Edge of the Land and in *amazement / awe / joy,* we watch this wonderful spectacle.

• o •
(End of Volume 1 of BOOK OF TRINITY)